Kindle Fire Ma

The Original Kindle Fire User Guide

Unleash EVERYTHING The Kindle Fire has to offer with this Kindle Fire Manual

By Sharon Hurley

Check out Sharon Hurley's User Guide for the Kindle Paperwhite!

Kindle Paperwhite User Guide: The Best Paperwhite Manual to Master Your Device

http://www.amazon.com/Kindle-Paperwhite-User-Guide-ebook/dp/B00AIQUGNW

Table of Contents

Chapter 1 – Introduction
Introducing the Kindle Fire — 6
Kindle, Featuring Android — 7
Variation in Kindle and Kindle Fire — 7
LCD vs. E Ink — 8

Chapter 2 – Getting Started
How to Set Up the Kindle Fire — 9
How to Deregister the Kindle Fire — 10
Managing a Kindle Account — 11
Buying Book on the Kindle Fire — 11
Find Free Books to Read — 12

Chapter 3 – The Kindle Fire Interface
Understanding the Kindle Fire User Interface — 13
Using Menus, Icons and Gestures — 13
Searching the Newsstand — 15
Tablet for Book Lovers — 15
Reading Books and Documents — 16
Using the Search Feature — 17
Removing Books from the Kindle Fire — 18
Using the Keyboard — 18

Chapter 4 – Apps, Apps, Apps!

Installing and Launching Amazon Apps   21
Installing New Apps   21
Other Resources to Download Apps   22
Launching and Uninstalling Apps   23
Popular Apps for the Kindle Fire   24

Chapter 5 – Multimedia

Downloading Music & Videos with Amazon Prime   26
Understanding Amazon Prime   26
Syncing Media with the Kindle Fire   27
Listening to Music   28
Finding and Downloading Videos   29
Additional Settings for Media Player   31
Amazon Prime Troubleshooting   32

Chapter 6 – Browsing the Web

Surfing the Internet on the Kindle Fire   34
Silk Browser   34
Settings in the Silk Browser   36

Chapter 7 - Email

Sending and Receiving Emails   39
Set Up, Collect and Send   39
Additional Email Settings   40

Chapter 8 – Additional Settings

Connectivity for the Kindle Fire	43
Kindle Fire Menu Bar	43
Maintaining Battery Life	44
Configuring Wireless Settings	45
Display Settings on the Kindle Fire	47

Chapter 9 - Security

Security on the Kindle Fire	48
Password for Lock Screen	48
Credential Storage	49
Setting Parental Controls	49
Updating and Resetting the Kindle Fire	50
Updating Software	51
Lost or Stolen Kindle Fire	52

Chapter 10 - Troubleshooting

Troubleshooting the Kindle Fire	53
Restarting the Tablet	53
Troubleshooting Apps and Games	54
Synchronization Issues	54
Lost Password	55
Conclusion	56

Chapter 1

Introducing the Kindle Fire

Welcome to a new world of consumer hardware, inviting users to experience a superior tablet capable of sending and receiving emails, browsing the internet and reading books through Kindle's software. Similar to other Kindle devices, the Kindle Fire is only 7.5 by 4.7 inches but the device's specifications make it quintessential for activities far beyond mere reading.

The 1024 by 600 multi-touch Gorilla Glass displays 169 pixels per inch with a range of 16 million colors. The Kindle Fire allows for 8 GB of storage to hold music, video clips and podcasts, among other types of data like documents. Currently, there is no mobile Internet variant but all devices have wireless capabilities. Each device also comes with a 3.5 mm headphone socket and a micro-USB 2.0 connector.

Unlike other Kindle devices, the Kindle Fire possesses the Android 2.3 Gingerbread operating system and combines it with the visual style of previous Kindles.

Kindle, Featuring Android

Essentially, the Kindle Fire is an Android tablet with special software to resonate with those familiar with the Kindle reader. Using this software, an existing Kindle account user can sign in or even create a new account. By using the Android operating system, consumers can download an assortment of games and apps through the Amazon App Store.

The Kindle Fire is ideal for media and video playback as well as downloading materials from Amazon Prime. With this new look, eBook readers can take advantage of Kindle books, comics and magazines directly on the tablet. While the Kindle application is not new as it's featured on Android phones, owners can focus on building a library instead of just adding the usual apps. It's also more affordable than many other tablets on the market today.

Variations in Kindle and Kindle Fire

With the release of the Kindle Fire, there is an assortment of eBook readers available: the Kindle Fire, the fourth generation Kindle and Kindle Touch, which is another touch-screen version. The Kindle Touch has a 3G variant and each device has Wi-Fi connectivity.

These former devices do not have the same capabilities or high specifications of the Kindle Fire. They are also not compatible with music and video, nor do they have the storage space or color display.

Standard Kindle readers are light and small enough to fit in a pocket. The main difference is within the display.

LCD Vs. E Ink

Perhaps the most obvious difference between the Kindle variations is the manner in which content is displayed to the viewer.

Traditional Kindles use E Ink, which is essentially a form of electronic ink that looks like paper and can display text on the screen without the use of backlight. On the contrary, those familiar with LCD displays may notice that these displays can occasionally cause headaches upon viewing.

E Ink devices do not have this problem, so readers can read for hours without negative effects. The Kindle Fire uses the LCD display in touchscreen format like many mobile phones and tablets. By using this new display, the Kindle Fire can also be used as a portable media device, which was the original intention when Amazon entered the tablet market.

Chapter 2

How to Set Up the Kindle Fire

After making the purchase, the first step is to turn on the Kindle Fire. A series of screens will emerge that help owners set up and register the device. This is the point that is essential for users to connect to a Wi-Fi network in order to properly register the device with Amazon.

-In the Connect to a Network list, use the touchscreen capabilities to tap onto an available network. The Kindle Fire will connect to the network and then users can choose the appropriate Time Zone. In some cases, users may have to enter a password to connect to a Wi-Fi network.

-Tap Select a Time Zone from the available list and then click Continue. For those in countries other than the United States, tap More for a larger list. After making a selection, use the Back button in the bottom-left corner to return to the Time Zone screen.

-Once the Register Your Kindle screen appears, current Amazon account users can enter account information, an e-mail address and a password in the fields provided. Users can deselect the Show Password box so that the password doesn't appear while typing to make sure no unintended viewers see the password.

-For those without an account, click New to Amazon to create an Account link. This link will move into the Create an Amazon Account screen. Enter information including name, e-mail address and password before pressing Continue.

-Finally, users must complete the registration. Some users will want to read the terms of registration. The next step is to tap the button that says, By Registering, You Agree to All of the Terms Found Here. After reading the registration, tap the Close button to return to the registration screen. Finally, tap Register. A final screen appears saying Welcome to Kindle Fire that includes the user's name. There is also another option in case the Kindle is not registered to the correct user that says Not Your Name. Click to change if necessary.

At this point, the Kindle Fire will update itself to the latest version. When the download finishes, tap the Get Started Now button to view more quick tips on the Kindle Fire.

How to Deregister a Kindle

For those new Kindle owners that bought their device from a previous customer or received used, there are options to deregister a Kindle Fire. In order to remove current settings, tap on Settings and then click More. Click More once more and then click on the My Account option. In this menu, click Deregister. This will delete prior credentials from the previous owner.

Managing a Kindle Account

After registering or adding an account to the Kindle Fire, it's time to manage the account through the Amazon website.

By clicking on the Your Account option, users can sign in to the Amazon website. On the left column, users can then tap the Your Kindle link to move to the next step. On this page, users will be able to view a listing of eBooks regarding their particular account. Within these options, Kindle Fire users can view other types of Kindle products that can be downloaded from the page. Examples include books, magazines and documents.

Under the Kindle Payment Settings option, users can add or remove payment types within their Kindle account. It's vital to have a valid card when making a purchase.

Buying Books on the Kindle Fire

Like any Kindle, the main reason for purchasing a tablet is for the reading capabilities. In order to get started, it's crucial to have a wireless network connection, an Amazon account with a credit or debit card linked to the account.

By tapping on the Books option in the virtual bookshelf on the Kindle home screen, account holders can be reading a best seller within a few seconds. From this point, the next step is to tap the Store option so the tablet moves into the browser and displays the Kindle store. Within the Store, there are currently over one million titles to choose from.

After finding a specific magazine or book, customers can use the Buy Now With One Click button to make an instant purchase. It's important to activate an account before using this option.

Finding Free Books to Read

Customers are not merely limited to buying books thanks to actions from the Amazon company. Many titles can actually be found for free to customers who are willing to look. Most classic books from historic authors can be found for free online.

One way to find free books is to use the search tool within the Kindle Store. However, this option often leads to customers searching for hours with little luck. By searching the Internet, customers will find that there are several websites that announce when new eBooks are free within the Kindle Store. Try a search such as "free books Kindle Fire," that uses key words to find free books.

Chapter 3

Understanding the Kindle Fire User Interface

Despite that the tablet was born within the realms of the Android 2.3, the Kindle Fire is much different than the typical Android system. Unlike the Android Gingerbread UI, the new interface is known as the Newsstand.

Within the newsstand, books and apps are listed in a way that allows for a finger or stylus to navigate between screens. In addition to this ease of navigation, users can also use a search tool that acts as a library index. Unlike other tablets, the main focus within the Kindle Fire is reading books, but searching the web and using apps are also possible for tech-savvy users.

Using Menus, Icons and Gestures

Initially, the user interface seems different than an Android device but there are also many similarities for an easy transition with the Kindle Fire.

One similarity exists within the Home button in the lower left corner. The Settings menu can be found by tapping the icon in the top right of the display. Opening the Settings menu allows users to adjust volume and brightness, connect to various Wi-Fi networks, sync books with Amazon, toggle the rotation lock and even provide access with more advanced settings.

In general usage, Kindle Fire owners will notice that the Home and Back button are the most frequently used buttons. The Back button is located in the center of the bottom of the display.

Similar to other touch screen tablets or smart phones, several gestures can be used in order to interact with the device. With a simple tap, users are replicating the familiar touch of the left click on a mouse for a desktop. By tapping and holding, owners will see a context menu of various options to choose from. By swiping on the screen, users can browse within the device for various content, especially useful in the Newsstand mode. By using the thumb and forefinger, users can also zoom in or zoom out by pinching or un-pinching the screen in the opposite direction.

Along the top of the screen, Kindle Fire owners will find their name across a narrow bar. The same bar displays the time, remaining battery and wireless connectivity signal. In addition to these basics, users can also access the Notification Area to learn about various apps and new emails. These notifications can be found in a grey disc, which can be expanded by clicking. After searching through new data, simply click the Clear All feature and then Home to go back. If the Kindle Fire goes into Sleep mode, simply tap the button in the lower edge of the tablet. This button is also the power button to switch the device off and on.

Searching the Newsstand

After pressing the Home button, users will be moved to the Newsstand, which is a virtual bookshelf where books and apps are located. By swiping left or right with a finger or stylus, users can scroll through shelves of materials. By using this carousel-like browser, users can find any item they may consider using. If a certain material isn't found immediately, users can browse other shelves below or use the search tool at the top of the tablet by keying in a key word or phrase.

Tablet for Book Lovers

A lifetime of books can easily fit onto the 8 GB of storage held on the Kindle Fire. Despite having a slightly different look than previous Kindles, the Kindle Fire is still meant to appease book lovers of all ages.

Because of the book-lover chromosome in the DNA of the Kindle Fire, the Newsstand is vital for holding books. The Newsstand provides a way for book lovers to find recent and familiar titles at any time, even on the go. On the Newsstand or Books menu, users can find titles to store on the device or in the Amazon cloud. Within the Cloud, books can be sorted alphabetically by Author, Recent or Title.

In order to launch a book for the first time, it's important to follow two steps. First, a user must download the publication by giving the book a single tap. Next, the user can click the cover illustration after the eBook has downloaded and presented itself on the tablet. Any book on the Kindle Fire can be moved to Favorites for a quick find. To do so, simply find the item and tap and hold to display the menu. On the menu, click the Add to Favorites feature to move the item into the Newsstand.

Reading Books and Documents

After opening a book on the tablet, turning a page is as simple as swiping a finger or stylus from left to right, or by tapping on the screen. To go back to the menu, users can tap on the bottom edge of the screen. From this point, the Home button and Back button will be revealed, along with Font Size options. Readers can also jump through the book to specific parts and there is also an Annotation button for readers to add notes or thoughts throughout the piece. In the menu, a Search tool is useful for finding specific phrases or sentences. These two features are great for students conducting research on historic works of literature.

While reading, there is a progress bar to let readers know which page they are currently on and where they are in the book. This bar also includes a slider that allows readers to move throughout the book.

In the top right corner, readers can find a grey bookmark. By tapping this page while reading, users can return to that particular page at any time during the reading. This is also helpful for those conducting research on a book.

Besides Kindle eBooks, there are other forms of documents that can be read on a Kindle Fire. Other forms have less menu options but these documents can still be read by using the pinch-to-zoom gesture, ideal for documents in the PDF format. On most documents, a double tap also zooms. Documents can be read in formats including Kindle Format 8, Kindle Mobi (.azw), txt, pdf, mobi, and prc. All of these documents can be enjoyed in full color on the LCD screen. Books and magazines in these formats can be copied to the Kindle Fire by using a USB cable.

Using the Search Feature

When using the Search feature outside of the book, the tool helps Kindle Fire owners search for books in any format, title or topic within the tablet. To use this feature, users simply tap into the Search box, which opens the Search page and gives results in the same area.

The Search feature can also be used to search the Internet by tapping on the Web button in the top right corner and keying in a search term. By tapping on the Library button, the search will then move back to focus on items in the tablet. Besides books and documents, apps and games can also be searched for by using this feature.

While reading a book, there is another search feature for users of the Kindle Fire. While in book view, readers can use the Search feature by tapping the magnifying glass Search button. It's important to type a long and accurate search phrase in the bar. To find the best results, it may take some time.

Removing Books from the Kindle Fire

Despite the large amount of space on the Kindle Fire, users will still decide to delete books purchased from the Kindle store that they have already read or perhaps didn't enjoy. Removing a book from the reader is quite simple.

To begin, open the Books section and find the title that needs to be removed. Use the Search tool if necessary. After finding the specific book, tap and hold until the Remove from Device option appears. From here, the book will disappear from the Kindle Fire, but it will still remain in the account of the Amazon cloud.

Using the Keyboard

Once a Kindle Fire owner understands the basics of the grips and gestures, it's time to engage the keyboard. The tablet is stocked with a software keyboard that displays on the screen; unlike previous Kindles that featured a keyboard within the hardware.

Generally, the keyboard is hidden and only reveals itself when information is necessary. The keyboard automatically appears when emails or forms are opened or when connected to Wi-Fi. The keyboard also appears if the Search box is opened or whenever a user taps within a text field.

When the keyboard opens, a standard QWERTY keyboard appears, along with a series of numbers from 1 to 0. Numbers are entered by either tapping the 123!? to the left of the Space bar, which will display a secondary keyboard to replace the first. This secondary keyboard will feature numbers and various forms of punctuation. There is also a third keyboard option available that displays math symbols. Pressing the ABC key can bring the main keyboard back.

Typing is as simple as using any keyboard, although the feel of the flat screen will be different at first. Using the backspace key on the top right corner of the keyboard can erase mistakes. The cursor can also be dragged to various points of the text by moving it with the finger on the top portion of the screen.

Copy and paste features are also available on the Kindle Fire. In order to select a word or phrase, users simply double tap on a selected word and tap it once more to display the Edit text menu. Within the Edit text menu, the Cut and Copy options appear. To paste or copy text, users long tap the text field and the Paste option will appear. There is also an Input Method on this same menu that allows for users to switch between the Kindle Fire keyboard and alternatives keyboards that can be purchased within the Amazon App Store.

Some users find the keyboard to be difficult because of the size of the individual keys and the unfamiliarity when compared to a typical computer keyboard. In both forms of the keyboard (portrait and landscape), nearly half of the screen is devoted to the keyboard. Because the screen is so large, some users have trouble seeing the other half of the screen. By using the scroll feature, users can move the non-keyboard part of the screen to see more or close the keyboard button by clicking a close option in the lower left corner of the screen. When the phrase or word is complete, the user simply presses the submit key in the lower right corner.

Chapter 4

Installing and Launching Amazon Apps

After setting up the Kindle Fire, users can spend leisure time enjoying books and magazines on a high speed, full color display. Besides the basic reading materials, users can install and launch apps from the Amazon App Store, which is an online marketplace for the device. The App Store can be reached from any wireless connection but there are some international restrictions.

Installing New Apps

Finding new apps is simple. Tap on Apps and then click on Store to browse available selections. When users see an app of interest, they can tap on the app to open a description page. From here, Kindle Fire users can find out details about the product, along with screenshots and even reviews from other users. In addition, the description page also gives recommendations for similar apps in the same genre.

After choosing an app, the next step is to install the app. Like downloading books, it's important to have a credit card linked to the Amazon account. View the price list on the app or description page and then tap on the Get App option. The download will complete in the background while the progress bar will have a status bar in the foreground.

Other Resources to Download Apps

Because not all Kindle Fire owners are in the United States, there are other services available to install apps and games. In order to do this, it's important to make sure the device is set up to install apps from a third party location.

In order to complete this task, Open Settings and then tap More, followed by Device. Switch Allow Installation of Applications from the default setting of Off to On. The tablet will inform the user that this action isn't safe but the choice is utterly up to owner of the device and must be done to download items from other locations.

While the Kindle Fire is trying to protect itself, there are several safe options for third party downloads. One of the most popular platforms is the Opera App Store, available at apps.opera.com in the Kindle Fire Browser. The Opera App Store accepts credit cards or PayPal as forms of currency to purchase apps. This platform works basically the same way by finding an app and clicking on the Download option.

After clicking the Download option, tap the Menu button in the middle of the browser toolbar and then select Downloads. From this point, there is a progress bar available to see the progress of the download. After the download completes, the user can tap on the completed app and begin the installation procedure. From here, there are more specific instructions set as guidelines.

Other resources such as andappstore.com, slideme.org and m.getjar.com work similarly. As a general guideline, it's wise not to install any apps that aren't currently available within the official Google Play store or the Amazon App Store.

Launching and Uninstalling Apps

After download any number of apps, there are two specific places to find these apps. On the Newsstand menu, there is an Apps screen where regularly used and new apps can be conveniently found. In the Newsstand, apps will be listed By Title or in order of most recently used. If users have any trouble finding a particular app, remember to use the Search tool to find any document, app or book. By scrolling up and down through the shelves, users can find all sorts of apps in the Newsstand.

The other way to launch apps is to use the main Newsstand screen. This screen displays the most recently used books, documents, games, apps and media files, which makes finding a particular app easy to find and use.

When an app is no longer useful or there is another reason the user wants to delete the app, uninstalling is quick and easy. By opening the Apps screen, users can long tap the app to be removed until a menu appears that allows users to Remove from Device. For those who wish to remove the app from the Newsstand rather than the entire tablet, this can be completed by tapping and holding until the menu says, Remove from Carousel, keeping it on the tablet and out of the way.

Popular Apps for the Kindle Fire

There is an assortment of great and useful apps that come standard on the Kindle Fire but there are also hundreds of others to choose from. For those looking for other great free apps within the Amazon App Store, the following will list a few free apps to download.

Evernote is a popular app that is used for note taking on the Kindle. *Pulse* is a newspaper app where users can actually tailor the app to specific interests. The *Read it Later* app is great for web browsers to use that want to save apps to read later while surfing the net. Finally, *Wi-Fi Analyzer* is an app that gauges hotspots in the area to make sure the Kindle if linked with the fastest Wi-Fi in the area. Other popular free apps include *Skype, Facebook, Twitter* and *LinkedIn*. These social apps are great for keeping up with friends and coworkers. The key is to explore the app store often to find the most suitable apps for each individual.

Chapter 5

Downloading Music and Videos with Amazon Prime

In addition to reading books and magazines in the home, office or anywhere else, the Kindle Fire also acts as a portable multimedia electronic. Since the Kindle Fire only holds 8 GB of data and most high definition videos require over a GB, Amazon Prime has been designed to work as digital distribution over a Wi-Fi network—streaming directly from a source to the tablet. Hence, the Kindle Fire is equipped with a media player that can play back music or videos on the device that are stored in a cloud-based system online.

Understanding Amazon Prime

Because the Kindle Fire is a product from Amazon, it not only works as an eBook reader but also works as a receiver for digital distribution. Many of the Amazon services come along with the Kindle Fire, including Amazon Prime, which is Amazon's answer to digital distribution.

Similar to other convenient businesses, Amazon Prime began as a subscription-based, free shipping program. The program quickly moved to include Amazon Instant Video, which allows streaming movies with the click of a mouse. The Instant Video feature includes television shows as well as movies and originally worked on the computer but is now set up to stream directly to the Kindle Fire.

An Amazon Prime membership allows for users to access the Kindle Owners' Lending Library, which allows users to borrow popular books like a brick-and-mortar library. These books have no specific due date but clients are limited to only having one book per month. For those who do not have an Amazon Prime account, it's as simple as logging onto the Amazon website and clicking on My Account to create a membership. From here, simply follow the onscreen instructions.

Syncing Media with the Kindle Fire

For those who wish to transfer various types of media to the Kindle Fire, it's as simple as attaching a USB cable. To transfer media without the use of a cable, Amazon Cloud Drive also provides music and media.

After connecting the device with a USB chord, the screen will change to display "You can now transfer files from your computer to your Kindle," that is displayed with a USB graphic image. The chord can be used for more than just music, it can also be used to copy books and videos directly to the Kindle Fire.

Once the cable is connected, open My Computer for Windows systems and find the tablet listed on the drive, which is usually listed as KINDLEFIRE. For other computers, the icon should appear on the screen or within the Finder window. Files can be moved from any folder on any computer as long as the file fits one of the styles that the Kindle Fire accepts. From the music folders on the computer, simply right click and select Copy. After completing this task, switch back to Kindle Fire folder on the computer screen and right click to select Paste.

After moving the files to the device, make sure to tap the Disconnect button before removing the USB cable to make sure the files have completed downloading. From here, users will be able to enjoy content on their portable Kindle Fire.

Listening to Music

After copying the music from the computer to the Kindle Fire, users can then play the music. In order to play a song, the user must click on the Music button within the Newsstand. The Search tool is available if a song or album is not immediately found. On the tablet, music is sorted by Playlists, Artists, Albums and Songs for ease of search.

Once the song or album is found, simply tap the title or album art to play a song. Like reading a book, a progress bar will appear that engages the listener to know the length of the song and allow the listener to pause or move through the song. Listeners can also control volume and move songs from repeat or random with the tap of the screen. For those who want to multitask on the Kindle Fire, it's as simple as tapping the Hide button on the music player. This button allows users to scroll through the Newsstand while listening to a favorite song or audiobook.

For those owners who have previously or wish to purchase music through Amazon, these songs can be downloaded and added through the Cloud Drive. By signing in with an Amazon account, users will see further instructions on loading Amazon-purchased music into the Cloud Drive. These particular songs can then be played in the Music screen of the tablet and songs will be listed under Cloud. These files must come in aac, mp3, midi, ogg and wav formats.

Finding and Downloading Videos

Unfortunately, moving video files and clips is different than syncing music. This problem occurs because of the specific formats that the Kindle Fire requires for video. For those who wish to sync videos, a third party system is required. PC owners using Windows can use an open source known as Miro media player. This particular program is available at www.getmiro.com.

After following the online steps, this media player will convert video clips to a proper viewing format suitable for the Kindle Fire. Like transferring music, simply connect the USB cable from the computer to the Kindle Fire. Here, open Miro and look for the tablet listed on the left side of the folder. In the app, a Video view will appear allowing for users to sync files by dragging files to the Kindle Fire and then to the Video folder on left side of the screen. It's important to remember that the Kindle Fire only holds 8 GB of storage, so it's important not to copy too many videos. The tablet will play MP4 and VP8 formats.

The Prime Instant Video service, established from Amazon Prime allows for account holders to choose from thousands of clips and videos. There are recommendations from Amazon and the program also offers unlimited streaming to all tablets. Besides thousands of video clips, the program offers new and popular movies that customers can rent or buy specifically for the Kindle Fire.

In order to begin watching video clips, simply tap Video and then tap Store. From here, users can choose a movie by reading ratings, descriptions and reviews from other users. To rent a movie, simply tap the Rental button along the right side of the tablet. For those who wish to purchase a movie, click the Buy button to keep the film within the Amazon Cloud. Kindle Fire owners also have the option to tap Add to Watchlist, where the user will be able to conduct further research to make a decision on whether to buy or a rent a movie. The final option would be to tap More Purchase Options, which offers a 24 Hour HD Rental, meaning that customers have a full day to watch the movie as often as they wish. After choosing to make a purchase or rental, the user can watch the movie immediately on the Kindle Fire screen.

Additional Settings for Media Player

Although the media player comes standard with preset settings, some users may want to adjust settings in the media player app. Within the Music and Video player, there are advanced options to fit all user needs.

For those who wish to access or change these presets, start by tapping the Menu button at the bottom of the window player. From here, tap Settings. In order to change the video options, there is an option called Disable HD purchase warning, where there will be an option to check a box meant to prevent users from purchasing HD videos that are more expensive than standard movies. This is also the area that allows for users to Clear Search History, meant to reset video search.

The music player offers more settings for Kindle Fire users to change. Here, customers can Enter a claim code from an Amazon Gift Card. Another option allows users to Clear cache, which actually speeds up search results and allows options for playback tracks. This allows for music to play with Lock-screen controls, which will allow playback on the Kindle Fire. In addition, another setting is the Enable equalizer modes, which offers a multitude of presets to give listeners exact settings.

Besides the basics, users can adjust Amazon Cloud Drive settings. One aspect of this feature allows users to decide where purchases will be saved directly on the tablet or in the Cloud Drive. Users can also adjust Delivery preferences or use Automatic Download options for all current and future downloads.

Another feature, which updates itself every ten minutes, is known as Refresh Cloud Drive. This feature functions by constantly updating the Cloud Drive. In addition to these advanced settings, users can manage media files on the Kindle Fire within the Video and Music players. In order to do so, simply tap and hold to display a context menu and read the steps to learn more. Here, users can remove tracks from the tablet that they no longer wish to hear.

Amazon Prime Troubleshooting

For those who are having trouble accessing Amazon Prime or using Prime Instant Video within the Cloud Drive, this happens because the program is currently not available outside of the United States. To fix this problem, users need a US-based postal address and an American credit card to key into the system.

Chapter 6

Surfing the Internet on the Kindle Fire

The multifunctioning device is not only set up for reading and playing media, but has fully functioning Internet connectivity. Unlike other Kindle browsers that were set to the default settings of limited to no Internet browsing, the Kindle Fire was created with Internet capabilities in mind. This tablet embraces the chance to engage in portable browsing at any available hot spot.

Silk Browser

Designed for speed, the Kindle Fire is ideal for working and surfing online. Thanks to a "split-browser" designed from Amazon, using the Internet is spit between the device and cloud servers for twice the speed. By clicking on the Web link within the Newsstand, users can access any website that can accessed by a computer. After clicking on the Web option, the browser gives users a new tab upon launch as well as a list of previously visited shortcuts. In addition to the regular websites, the page also displays an address bar for visiting new websites.

In the address bar at the top, users can key in an entire URL or use the bar as a search tool by entering a phrase or key word. For those who wish to use another type of search, a number of search engines can be used in this bar as a default. In addition to the search bar, there is a Refresh button in the upper right corner of the page. Above these bars, there is a + button that allows users to open additional tabs.

The Silk Browser uses the most of the screen. At the button of the screen, users can return to a previous page by simply pressing the Back button. In addition to finding the Back button, users can also press the Full Screen option to maximize the page for ultimate Internet viewing. While browsing websites, the address bar will disappear from the top of the screen but it can be found again by simply scrolling to the top of the page.

Next to the Back button, on the right, users will find a Bookmarks button to add favorite websites that they wish to view again. There is also another option where websites can be added by tapping the Add bookmark button for a quick add.

Besides the visible buttons, there is a Menu option on the center of the toolbar, in the lower edge of the screen that offers added features. In addition to the Add bookmark button, the menu also offers a Share page feature, that allows for those surfing the net web to share a URL through either chat, email or even *Facebook* (in addition to other social apps on the Kindle Fire). The Downloads button shows current downloads within the browser and Settings opens another

35

screen with further configurations. Finally, the Clear All button will delete the search history.

Settings in the Silk Browser

Besides the default settings, there are several advanced options to adjust the Silk Browser for each viewer. Within the Settings screen, users can clear the cache, enable or disable Flash and JavaScript in webpages and even adjust search engines between organizations like *Google, Yahoo*, and *Bing* by tapping on Set search engine in the menu.

In the Settings screen, various sections help to group the different categories. There are also settings including Text size where users can decide between using zoom or Auto-fit pages to show specific dimensions to display images and web pages proportionally. By disabling this feature, Internet search can be faster.

Also in the menu, the Saved Data button encompasses all downloaded materials. In this setting, users can Accept cookies, which is vital for an Amazon device. Also in the menu, users can Clear all cookie data and Clear cache, which erases databases and temporary files. Finally, by tapping the Clear history button, users can clear the entirety of visited pages. For those who complete several forms on a regular basis, there is an option to tap on Remember form data to save items regularly inserted within a form.

However, some users will want to disable this feature for security reasons. A similar feature would be the Remember password option, but this is also not always wise for security reasons since the device is portable. For those who wish to disable these options, it's possible to Clear password to empty these stored passwords in the Silk Browser.

Under the Behavior settings, there are additional features involving security. Websites that have security features will be flagged by default. The Show security warnings checkbox can be cleared but this is not an ideal option. Flash and JavaScript can enhance or lengthen the browsing experience so this decision will often depend on the user and types of websites regularly viewed. These functions help to decide issues involving the look of a page or video streaming capabilities. The reason to possibly block these abilities is because advertisers also use these features so some users will want to disable in order to avoid excess advertisements. Kindle Fire users can also Block pop-up windows by choosing to pick either Ask, Never or Always.

In the Advanced section, users can tap on Accelerate page loading but it's important to understand this may be canceled out from those also using Optional encryption. All web pages can be viewed in either Desktop or mobile view—the option is truly up to the viewer to decide a preference. Text encoding should be left to default unless Kindle Fire owners need to display a website in another language that involves a separate alphabet. Finally, Website settings are meant to adjust the behavior of regularly visited websites and they can actually empty the amount of data stored on the device rather than in the Cloud.

Chapter 7

Sending and Receiving Emails

When tablets hit the market, businessmen and students were excited to have a portable emailing device, with sending and receiving capabilities. These emails can also have attachments that even include photos.

By providing email functions, the Kindle Fire has the same capabilities of other tablets and smartphones. This is ideal for keeping in touch with friends and co-workers at any moment and being able to respond all hours of the day. The Kindle Fire can access personal and corporate email accounts. Unlike former devices, the Kindle Fire has complete email configuration for accounts like *Gmail*, *Hotmail* and other accounts. In the Advanced settings, users can configure the Kindle Fire to appease any email account to keep in touch with all friends, family and coworkers.

Set Up, Collect and Send

After properly setting up the Silk Browser, users can load emails. In the Apps screen, the Kindle Fire has an Email app available that can support several accounts for those with multiple emails or for anyone sharing a tablet with family or spouse. After launching this app, the user will be asked to key in an account name along with a password.

Most of the settings are available through a default method but users can change any settings by tapping Menu and then Accounts. In order to switch between accounts, there is a switch in the drop down menu in the upper left corner of the screen within the email app.

After keying in the correct information, email messages will appear in the inbox. By tapping on any of these messages, users can read and reply to any particular message. Messages can also be forwarded just like using a computer. In order to send a message, simply tap on the Compose button in the menu of the email app and type the email address of whoever is meant to receive the message. For those who wish to send multiple messages, simply tap on the Cc/Bcc button to send to any number of intended recipients. Make sure to enter a subject into the Subject line and make sure to click the Save Draft button while writing long emails that may take time to finish. After typing the message, simply tap the Attach button to add an image or file to the document being sent. Make sure to be familiar with the keyboard and typing messages from the Kindle Fire will be simple. Once the message is complete, simply tap Send to mail the message to the recipient.

Additional Email Settings

For those who want more than default settings, there are options available to change the email app on the Kindle Fire. One change involves the Check for messages button that rests in the middle of the menu bar on the email app. This button actually overrides default settings to allow for users to decide whether they want to manually check for messages or have message alerts. There is also a Search tool on the menu bar that allows for users to search for specific messages within the email account. There is a sorting option in the top right section of the screen that is set on Newest, but allows for users to decide how the Inbox is arranged. Other options include Sender, Subject, and Attachments.

Also on the menu button, there is a list of Contacts associated with each email account. The Kindle Fire will automatically sync a user's list of contacts from their email account. The Folders button also provides users with other folders such as Outbox and Sent items. These are ideal when using a multitude of devices for email services. The Settings button gives a few more options to create a personal email experience.

After tapping on the Settings option, users can choose an Account name and decide which is used as the Default account. Within these settings, users can choose whether or not images are automatically shown in emails. By tapping on Always show images the user can choose Yes or No. Choosing No is ideal for accounts that get a great deal of spam messages. For those who wish to see images from friends but not spam, there is an option to choose images From contacts or From anyone, which helps to specify which images are received.

From this same menu, there is an option to decide how often the Kindle Fire checks for new messages in the Inbox. By tapping the Fetch new messages option, users can choose between Manually, Hourly, Every 15 minutes or Every 30 minutes to decide how often messages are checked. Kindle Fire owners can also decide whether or not they wish for messages to be deleted from the tablet or from the server. The When I delete option gives two chooses that are Do not delete on server or Delete from server. Finally, users can choose standard or encrypted email collections by configuring the Incoming mail server option.

Additional settings can be adjusted in the Sending mail section, allowing for users to choose items like Composition defaults. Here, Signatures can be added to all outgoing messages or users can decide between From and Bcc. Messages can also be switched between Plain text or HTML, but Plain text changes formatting and removes images when a message has been replied to. Another adjustment lies in the Quote original message when replying, which can be toggled on or off. The Outgoing server can also be changed to a user's particular configurations. Finally, Notifications can be silenced or aligned with a particular sound in the Settings screen and each Folder can be aligned for a different purpose.

Chapter 8

Connectivity for the Kindle Fire

After learning the ins and outs of the Kindle Fire, some users will choose to change a few of the default settings in the behavior of the tablet. While most of the settings are somewhat permanent, there are options available in a hidden settings menu. Within the hidden menu, users can manage screen rotation and adjust how the tablet connects in wireless networks as well as how the battery is used in the device.

Kindle Fire Menu Bar

In the Kindle Fire's interface, there are two main menus used to change various aspects within the device. All of the apps and books have a menu at the bottom of the screen to help users navigate throughout the device, known as the toolbar. The other menu is the settings menu that is hidden from day to day usage. For those who are looking for the menu, however, it is easy to find. By tapping the Settings button in the top right of the screen, users can access the second menu. The secondary menu allows for users to open five different settings not presented in the bottom menu.

-The Locked setting can be toggled for users to decide whether or not the screen rotates with viewing or stays standard.

-The second adjustment is the Volume, which can be adjusted by sliding the finger along a line of volume.

-The next setting is Brightness, which changes the backlighting on the screen. This setting is ideal for those who wish to read the Kindle Fire in different levels of exterior lighting. By having the brightness turned down, users can also preserve battery life.

-The Wi-Fi setting allows for users to configure general set up and connectivity options.

-Finally, the Sync button allows for users to sync the Kindle Fire with a particular Amazon account. By default, this feature will sync every ten minutes.

Maintaining Battery Life

Because the Kindle Fire is a portable device, it relies on a rechargeable battery for power supply. A full charge can generally last a day but the power life span is shortened with frequent usage. Perhaps the largest power requirement is when using Amazon Instant Video to stream movies or television shows. However, there are ways to preserve battery life.

The first step is to make sure the Kindle Fire is being charged correctly. One way is to attach the Kindle Fire to a computer by using a USB chord, but this is not the most effective way. It's best to use the wall charger that comes with the device and allowing for the tablet to have a full recharge that will take a few hours. This should be done once a week and the tablet should be left to charge for at least four hours.

For those who have the brightness at full level or who may be using full volume, the battery will seem to drain quickly. It's important to keep these settings at low and appropriate levels. Another issue is within the wireless network. When the Kindle Fire is having problems connecting with a weak connection, the battery will be drained. When using the device in weak signal areas, it's a good idea to disable the Wi-Fi to save battery. In addition, battery is also drained when downloading or syncing large files. Generally, the Kindle Fire battery life should last up to eight hours when reading and at least seven for video playback (as long as Wi-Fi is disabled).

Configuring Wireless Settings

Also within the Settings menu, located at the top right of the screen, users can choose a wireless network. By switching Wi-Fi to On, the device will automatically scan the area for a wireless signal. By tapping on a Wi-Fi network, users can join the network and begin using the Internet. Some networks require a password and the password option will pop up after clicking on the selected network. Passwords must be acquired from the owner of the wireless router, whether this individual is a homeowner or business employee. To enter the address, simply click within the text box and a keyboard will appear. By tapping the Show password checkbox, users can see the letters that are being keyed in. Otherwise, it's safer to not check this option and keep the password hidden from wandering eyes. After keying in the password, simply tap Connect and let the tablet connect with the selected network.

Once the device has connected to a network, there are further details that can be adjusted on the tablet. To change default settings, tap on the network name to see a status, along with link speed, signal strength and security options. Users can also examine the IP address for any networking problems that may arise from the router.

Under the Advanced Settings, Kindle Fire owners can choose to Use static IP, which is useful for those with frequent router problems at home or who suffer from problems in frequent Wi-Fi hotspots. Several options, including IP address specifications are available. Users can also adjust Subnet Mask and choose between DNS numbers. This portion allows for users to Add Networks, which is crucial for connecting to those networks that are undetected or hidden for whatever reason. For this to be done, users must have a correct Network SSID, which will depend on various security types. There are six options available that range from Open to WPA2 EAP. From here, click Save to connect.

For those who connect to a large number of wireless networks, this can result in a long list of networks to make reconnecting quick and easy. To reduce the list, simply tap on any of the networks within the list and then tap Forget.

Display Settings on the Kindle Fire

Brightness can be found in another area besides the hidden Settings menu button in the top right of the screen. The Brightness can also be adjusted by tapping on Settings, then More, then Display. This is also where users can find the Screen Timeout button that allows for the tablet to delay before the screen switches off. Options range between 30 Seconds to 1 Hour and there is also a Never button that is vital for watching long video files.

Chapter 9

Security on the Kindle Fire

Because tablets can be connected to the Internet and may hold personal data along with credit card information, it's important to keep the Kindle Fire protected. The lock screen can be assigned an encrypted password and parental controls can also be given to keep children from accessing the device without an adult.

Password for Lock Screen

When the Kindle Fire is turned on or awakened from sleep mode, the Lock Screen appears. In this standby mode, there are default settings randomly displayed. This feature protects the Kindle Fire from accidently being turned on or from any of the apps running unexpectantly that may run down power on the tablet. There are two types of lock screen variations available. To change between these options, visit Settings and then click More, followed by tapping Security. From here, tap Lock Screen Password and decide between Tap or Drag to combine a password of four characters for the tablet.

Password options are flexible and can be composed of letters, character and numbers. After choosing and confirming a password, users can test the password by tapping the power button and switching it to standby, followed by tapping the power button again to wake the tablet. In order to disable a password, the password must be entered beforehand. It's important to know that when a password is entered incorrectly four times, the Kindle Fire must be reset.

Credential Storage

For those with Microsoft Exchange-based accounts, there is a Credential Storage option available within the Security Screen. This does not apply to most users but for those that do need such a feature, the network administrator is necessary for configuration. Within the Security Screen, tap on Install Secure Credentials, Set Credential Storage Password and Use Secure Credentials. To reset any of these options, tap Clear Credential Storage.

Setting Parental Controls

Because children are as attracted to electronics as adults, it's vital to have a safety lock on all tablets. Various websites are too adult for children and because of the possibility of having a credit card linked with various apps, it's wise to protect the Kindle Fire from children who may wish to explore the device. By tapping Settings, then More, then Parental controls, users can decide whether to toggle the button to On or Off. This feature protects the tablet from both children and potential thieves who many tamper with the tablet. Using Parental Controls helps to restrict certain purchases and keep others from visiting inappropriate websites or accessing content that should not be accessed. After activating the Parental Control, the device will only be able to be used for those who know the secure password.

Updating and Resetting the Kindle Fire

Whether users are purchasing a used Kindle or giving one as a gift, there is an option to reset the Kindle Fire for new owners. Some may wish to simply update the Kindle Fire while others may want to completely reset the device.

For those who wish to change an account, this requires deregistering the tablet. To deregister a Kindle Fire, simply tap on Settings, then More, then tap on My Account. From here, users can deregister the previous account and begin to assign a new account holder. New Amazon accounts can be keyed in or completely new accounts can be created. It's possible to then sync the tablet with previously purchased content and media. Please review the opening chapters of this guidebook to find out more about how to properly set up a Kindle Fire.

It's important to remember that when changing owners, all of the previous data that has been downloaded or synced from another account will be removed from the tablet. This will not erase data from the Cloud, merely the tablet. To find out which forms of media are on the tablet, click on Settings, then More, then My Account and finally, tap Device. This will display all data held on the device.

Storage is divided between Application Storage and Internal Storage where the Application portion holds 1.17 GB and the Internal holds 5.36 GB. It's a good idea to occasionally check this data to find out what is being held on the device and what can be deleted. New users who do not want to reset the Kindle can check here to decide what to keep and what to erase.

For new owners to feel the entire personal touch of the Kindle Fire, it's best to Reset the device. In the Device window, move down and tap the option that reads, Reset to Factory Defaults. Since this step is so detrimental to the device, a confirmation will arise to confirm this is truly the option the user wishes to perform. Also, the device will need at least forty percent battery to perform this feature. Despite the severity of the action, the reset is a fairly quick procedure. For those who think there may be additional data on the device, they can simply plug the tablet to a computer using a USB and manually erase any media within the Video, Music, Books, Pictures or Documents folders on the Kindle Fire.

Updating Software

By continually updating the Kindle Fire's software, the owner can expect maximum functionality, as it will always run on the most up-to-date software. In order to keep up with new software, make sure to receive all Over the Air updates by occasionally signing onto wireless networks. Generally, the Kindle Fire will prompt users to update the software for the operating system.

For those who do not consistently receive update notifications, there is another option to update software. Tap Settings, then More, then My Account and then tap on Device. There will be an option to choose Update your Kindle where the tablet will be able to check for updates and then download and install these updates. The updates will only take a few minutes and then the user can surf or read on the most advanced version of the Kindle Fire.

Lost or Stolen Kindle Fire

In case of an accidental loss or chance of thievery, there are immediate steps to take to make sure the account has been disassociated with the tablet so no one can use an account that they do not own. Visit http://www.amazon.com/manageyourkindle to Deregister the device and erase any liability. Besides taking this action, it's a good idea to cancel any online magazine or book subscriptions to make sure no more money is lost with a missing a tablet.

Chapter 10

Troubleshooting the Kindle Fire

When problems arise, it's important to solve them quickly for a quick-loading, efficient tablet. Sometimes, the device may have some lag time between screens or with certain apps or games. Usually, this is involved with poor battery management, which can be solved by providing the Kindle Fire with a full charge. However, there are several other tips to remember for the most efficient tablet.

Restarting the Tablet

On the rare occasion that the tablet locks up, an app fails or the tablet freezes, it's important to respond accordingly. If users are unable to return to the Newsstand for any reason, it may be time to turn it off for a moment. There are two ways to restart the device.

-Before taking any action, it's important to decide whether or not the tablet has enough energy for a reboot. Sometimes, the tablet may be performing some process in the background, which is causing the battery to run low. If the battery is low, it's a good idea to charge the battery for half an hour before running a Hard Reset. If possible, perform the normal reset procedure by holding down the power button until the Shut Down button appears.

-If the device is completely frozen, the only way to reset the Kindle Fire is to hold down the power button for at least twenty seconds. From here, simply turn the tablet back on and the issue should be resolved.

Troubleshooting Apps and Games

Most problems with the Kindle Fire are associated with apps and it's best to examine the apps' settings to determine what is causing the particular problem. To do so, investigate the app and check the settings within the app. Disable any options that may be causing a problem.

If nothing changes after disabling a plausible option, tap Settings, More and then Applications. From here, find the app that is causing problems and use the Filter from the drop down menu if necessary to search. Check on the Storage of the app and then examine the app's Cache. If all else fails, check Defaults and Permissions. For an immediate improvement, it's vital to use the Force Stop button and then Clear Data, Clear Cache and Clear Defaults. If nothing seems to work, it may be time to Uninstall the app completely. Check the app store to see if others are having similar issues with a troublesome app.

Synchronization Issues

One particular frustrating problem comes from syncing books from the Amazon Cloud to the Kindle Fire. This may happen when various Kindle devices are assigned to one Amazon account—whether there are several tablets or various smartphones registered. One issue will resolve with missing pages from a downloaded book. Usually, missing pages are in fault due the book's author. If a user encounters this issue, it's ideal to Report the book on the Kindle Store product listing.

Other issues that arise from improper book downloading can be fixed by restarting the device or simply disconnecting and then reconnecting the Wi-Fi. Other problems that may occur happen when opening a book on the tablet. This can be fixed by opening the Books list and long tapping the book before finally selecting the Remove from Device option. From here, click the Cloud view and tap the book again to re-download. If this problem continues, Restart the device.

Lost Password

For those who have decided to secure a device with a screen lock password, it's possible to occasionally forget the code. For a lost password, the only option is to restore the device to the original factory settings. If this happens, the device will delete all personal data and content until it is properly registered again. From here, users can download former books from the Amazon Cloud. If a new password is assigned, make sure to make it memorable.

Conclusion

Now it's time to begin enjoying the Kindle Fire. With new features superior to previous tablets, the Kindle Fire is small and flexible as it creates a great user experience, allowing for users to carry thousands of books, songs or videos to any location and search the Internet freely at all available hotspots.

3592474R00031

Printed in Great Britain
by Amazon.co.uk, Ltd.,
Marston Gate.